# 館長序

隸屬於財團法人朱銘文教基金會的朱銘美術館，不僅完整收藏了朱銘先生各個時期的作品，亦典藏許多國內外知名藝術家之名作，自開館以來，我們在有限的經費下持續加強軟、硬體建設，積極籌辦各項展覽與推廣藝術教育相關活動，以期能提供參觀者更優質的美術館參觀經驗。

從十五歲開始，朱先生與廟宇雕刻師李金川老師學習傳統雕刻技藝，在近三年的學徒生涯中，朱先生練就了純熟的雕刻技法，此也奠定了日後由傳統雕刻轉入現代雕塑的好基礎。二十出頭時，在家鄉朱先生已是頗有名氣之木雕師傅，但是他亦漸漸地不能滿足工藝師傅所做的工作。1968年，朱先生辛苦地求得第二位恩師－楊英風先生，而與其說是向楊老師學藝術，不如說是「透過與楊老師一同生活，自然地體驗藝術。」在楊老師的帶領下，朱先生逐步跨進了現代藝術的領域。

1976年在國立歷史博物館所展出的鄉土系列作品以其粗曠且精準的刀法獨樹一格，更因當時文化界正熱烈宣揚鄉土運動，使朱銘先生受到大眾的矚目與討論。太極系列的發表則使其受到國際的肯定，學習太極拳多年，在其對太極精神的領悟與熟稔的雕刻技法雙重之配合下，讓太極系列作品充分表現了中國太極拳所強調內蘊的氣與外顯的勢；而近期人間系列作品，人的百態抽樣表現則是朱銘先生認為最貼近現代生活且能毫無束縛地進行創作的主題。

朱先生是一位創作力豐富並且不斷向自我挑戰的藝術家，在各式各樣創作材料的嘗試過程中，其藉由材質的轉變來磨練自己，因為他認為每一種材質有著屬於自己的特性是其他材質無法取代的，必須運用不同工具和不同的方式來與材質溝通。因此您在朱銘美術館內，您將發現各種材質所創作出的作品，不論是木雕、石雕、陶塑、海綿鑄銅、保利龍鑄銅、不鏽鋼等，雖呈現出截然不同的效果，卻都蘊含了創作者旺盛的生命力。

由於朱銘先生一向不喜歡用過多的話語來解釋自我的創作，所以在這本導覽手冊中，我們整理了許多知名藝評家對朱先生不同時期中各系列作品的評論或者對其本人的採訪資料，希望參觀者在親自欣賞朱先生的作品之餘，能有多一些的訊息來協助了解更多的作品內涵。此外，對於朱銘先生畢生最大的創作朱銘美術館的各項規劃、建設以及其它典藏作品的紹亦部分地收錄在這本導覽手冊中，我們企盼參觀者能透過本導覽手冊對朱銘先生及美術館有更深入的認識，也希望讀者能給予館方各項指導與批評，讓美術館一天天地進步與成長。

館長

朱原利

## Preface

Administered by the Juming Culture and Education Foundation, the Juming Museum is home to an integral collection of Ju Ming's work throughout his career. One can also find here the masterpieces of renowned artists from Taiwan and around the world. Since first opening our doors, we have steadily developed the facilities and services of the museum as our limited budget allows. We have also held a number of exhibitions and education activities in art to enrich the experience of our visitors.

At the age of 15, Mr. Ju began his three-year apprenticeship in traditional temple woodcarving under the master craftsman Lee Chin-chuan. It was during this period that he developed the carving skills that would form the foundation for his development from traditional woodcarving to modern sculpture. By the age of 20 he was already a master woodcarver of considerable accomplishment. But the work of a craftsman would not satisfy his ambition for long. In 1968, Mr. Ju went to great lengths to find a new teacher, a search that ended at the door of renowned sculptor Yuyu Yang. Of this second apprenticeship, he says that he did not so much learn art from Mr. Yang as, "experience art naturally by living with him." It was under Mr. Yang's guidance that Mr. Ju succeeded in crossing over to the world of modern art.

The 1976 exhibition of nativist sculptures at the National Museum of History in Taipei propelled Mr. Ju into the public spotlight. His work was critically acclaimed for both its singularly raw yet refined treatment and its coincidence with a renewed interest in nativist themes in Taiwan's art community at that time. With the subsequent unveiling of the Taichi Series, Mr. Ju was confirmed as an artist of international standing. In the Taichi Series sculptures, he joined an understanding of the spirit of taichi boxing, acquired from years of practice, with a consummate skill in sculpting, to vividly convey the harbored energy and external power of this Chinese martial art form. In his more recent Living World Series, Mr. Ju has gone on to explore the many faces of modern life under a theme allowing broad creative latitude.

Ju Ming joins an unusually creative talent with a commitment to constant self-challenge as an artist. He has experimented with every conceivable material in his work and grown with each transition to new media. He believes that each material possesses unique and inimitable qualities, requiring an artist to adopt equally unique tools and approaches to establish a dialogue with it. Visitors to the Juming Museum will therefore discover works made of all manner of materials, among them wood, stone, ceramic, foam rubber and stainless steel. Each conveys an entirely different effect, though all share in common the abundant vitality of their maker.

Ju Ming has never liked talking a lot about his own work, and thus this guidebook relies for its sources on the impressions of Mr. Ju's work by renowned art critics and interviews of the artist himself. The planning and construction of Mr. Ju's most ambitious creation, the Juming Museum, as well as works by other artists in the museum collection are also introduced within these pages. We hope that these insights can provide our visitors with a better understanding of the art of Ju Ming and enrich their experience at the museum.

Calvin Ju
Director of Juming Museum

# ［目錄］

# Contents

## How Juming Museum was established

打造一座 美術館

座落於山林間的朱銘美術館，蘊藏朱銘先生畢生的創作和對藝術的執著，從草建之初就堅持獨資不願受外力干預，朱先生毅然擔起所有工程細節，十二年來慢慢開採出一片天地。朱銘最初買地整地，只是為了解決大型作品存放的問題，結果發現矗立綠地中的雕塑別具韻味，就這樣引發他打造一座美術館的決心，於是在一九九九年九月十九日，寫進台灣藝術史的朱銘美術館誕生了！

朱銘美術館的寬闊戶外展場和沒有距離的展示方式，是全台絕無僅有的。在藝術品和綠地間穿梭，感受人文和大自然運轉交鋒的悸動，對許多參觀者來說是難得的經驗；也只有這樣的空間，才能忠實呈現朱銘作品裡蘊含的蕩然氣魄。自開幕以來，朱銘美術館不僅提供靜態的展示，更企劃一系列的藝術表演，從戲劇、說唱到音樂，目的在鼓勵參觀者和不同藝術形式間的互動，更回應了朱銘先生「活的美術館」的理念。

美術館地下一

Located amongst trees and hills, Juming Museum houses all the creative works by Ju Ming. From the construction phase of the museum, Mr. Ju insisted that the museum had to be funded by him only and that he would be responsible for all the details and construction himself. Originally, the building and area were intended to only house all his works, but later he found that the unique setting of the natural surroundings could enhance the artistic perception and appreciation of his sculptures. Therefore, he decided to turn the area into a museum. After 12 years of effort, the whole area has been transformed into a museum. On September 19, 1999, JUMING MUSEUM, which has been recorded in the Taiwan arts history, opened to the public.

Juming Museum is the first museum in Taiwan with such a broad outdoor exhibition, which enables visitors to look at Mr. Ju's works at a very close distance. Visitors to the museum can enjoy the works and feel the heartbeat of the Mother Nature at the same time. Only such a setting and broad area can bring out the essence and spirit of Mr. Ju's works. Since opening to the public, besides exhibiting Mr. Ju's works, the museum also has other artistic performances, including dramas, singing and music performances, thus allowing visitors to experience different types of arts. As Ju Ming said, "This is a live museum."

Ju Ming's life  and his art

# 朱銘的藝術 與人生

JUMING MUSEUM

# 朱銘的藝術與人生
## Ju Ming's life and his art

## 藝術的種子萌芽了

朱銘本名朱川泰，生於一九三八年的苗栗小鎮一通霄，在家排行十一。小時候家境窮困，父親朱李記因為身體不好，能工作的日子有限，母親得熬夜編織大甲蓆，才能勉強維持一家開銷。體貼的朱銘小學畢業後，就放棄升學的機會，開始工作貼補家用。朱銘十五歲那一年，通霄鎮上為了翻修媽祖廟，請來雕刻師李金川，朱李記看上李師傅的好手藝，特地帶了么兒上門拜師，朱銘就此開始他數十年的雕刻生涯。

二十出頭的朱銘，在家鄉開設了「海洋雕刻社」，工作之餘，他開始研究寫實風格的雕刻，為妻子刻的「玩沙的女孩」雕像，是這一時期的代表作。往後的幾年，朱銘度過了一段事業失利的艱苦日子，工廠結束營業之後，他帶著家人搬到大甲，努力工作還債，心裡始終還是懸著成為真正藝術家的念頭。

在三十歲的當口，朱銘進入楊英風門下學習，當時技術對他來說，早就不是問題，楊老師引領他在觀念上的轉變，讓朱銘從一個雕刻師脫身成為藝術家。他在這段期間的創作雖然出自鄉土題材，卻轉而有了現代雕塑的風貌。

## The budding young artist

The birth name of Ju Ming was Ju Chuan-tai. Born in 1938 at Tunghsiao of Miaoli in Taiwan, he was the 11th child of his family. In his childhood, his family was quite poor. His father, Ju Lee-chi, could work only intermittently due to infirmity, and his mother had to earn additional money by weaving straw mats until late at night most days. After Mr. Ju graduated from elementary school, he chose to start working in lieu of continuing his schooling in order to bring in extra money for his family. When he was 15 years old, a famous wood craftsman, Lee Chin-chuan, was invited to go to Tunghsiao to restore the Matsu Temple. Mr. Ju Lee-chi recognized that Mr. Lee was an outstanding craftsman, so he brought his youngest son, Ju Ming, to be the apprentice of Mr. Lee. That was the beginning of Ju Ming's sculpture life.

In his early 20s, Ju Ming ran the Ocean Sculpturing Studio in his hometown. When he had extra time off work, he studied the realist sculpture art. His work, A Girl Playing with Sand, in which his wife posed as the model, is a good representation of his work for that period. After a few years, he underwent a lot of hardship due to financial problems. After his factory closed down, he and his family moved to Dajia of Taichung in the middle of Taiwan. Though working quite hard for clear all his debts, he always had one goal—to be a real artist.

A few years later, when he was 30, he became a pupil and protégé of the famous artist, Yuyu Yang. By that time, Mr. Ju had mastered all the sculpture techniques, but then he was gradually transformed into a real artist from a skilled craftsman, through the artistic concepts, inspiration, guidance and furtherance obtained from Mr. Yang. A few years after that, although his works were focused on the subjects and scenes of nativist and plain folks, we can see that those works were with a touch of modern sculpture concept.

▲ 朱銘十五歲拜李金川為師，學習雕刻之情景，右三是朱銘， 臉被前面的同學遮了一半。
This photo shows Ju Ming, at the age of 15, learning sculpturing from Mr. Lee Chin-chuan. The third person from the right is Ju Ming, with his face partially blocked by another student.

▶ 民國五十二年朱銘在通霄鎮上成立了「海洋雕刻社」，閒暇之餘開始研究較有藝術性的雕刻手法。
In 1963, Ju Ming established Ocean Sculpturing Studio at Tunghsiao of Miaoli. When he had extra time off work, he started to study artistic sculpture techniques and concepts.

▶ 海洋雕刻社的徒弟們學習的情形。
The photo depicts Ju Ming's pupils learning by actually sculpturing at the Ocean Sculpturing Studio.

## 藝術家朱銘

一九七六年，楊英風以來不及準備為理由，將自己在歷史博物館的展覽檔期讓給朱銘。這次的個展成功地將朱銘推進台灣藝壇，而當時文化界的鄉土運動正如火如荼的進行著，朱銘與洪通被視為這個風潮中的代表人物。木雕太極也在這個展覽中悄悄出現，但是「水牛」等鄉土的表現題材被認為是代表本土風味的作品，才是那時眾人注目的焦點。

朱銘最初開始學太極，是因楊老師的建議為了強健體魄。他一本專注執著的性格，從學習的過程裡領悟到太極的精神，自然而然地，也就成為他創作的題材。經由七〇年代在亞洲的一系列個展，太極雕塑為他在亞洲藝壇奠下基礎。不斷為自己開創新局的朱銘，於一九八一年遠赴紐約尋求發展，他橫剖自己生存的世代，在陌生的城市裡孕育出另一個系列—人間，「人間系列—彩繪木雕」在此首次發表。

▲ 水牛，1979，木，Wood 62×33×32 公分
Buffalo, 1979, Wood, 62×33×32 cm

這個系列發展到後來演變成一場材質實驗的開發與探索；「海綿翻銅」採用繩子捆綁海棉製作模型，翻製成的青銅作品出乎意料的飽滿有彈性，成功地演繹出運動員的形象。自八〇年代中期開始，朱銘的創作觸角遍及拼貼、水墨、陶塑、石雕、以及最近的不銹鋼；由於一直環繞在「人」這個主題上，從太極雕刻之後的這些創作，全都歸在「人間系列」之下。

朱銘是個純真勇敢的人，藝術對他而言是種信仰，任何念頭一在他腦裡定案，就是真理，就得實行；一如楊英風當年的期許，朱銘以他幾近固執的堅持，在台灣的藝術史中佔下一席之地。

楊英風肖像，1993，木，45×37×56 公分
Portrait of Yuyu Yang, 1993, Wood, 45×37×56 cm

## 呦呦 楊英風

楊英風於1926年生於台灣宜蘭，一生致力推廣環境雕塑及生態美學，他的雕塑，特別是不銹鋼雕塑，意圖表達人和大自然相應相融的關係。英文的 Landscape 只限於一部份眼睛可見的風景或土地的外觀，而楊英風提倡的 Lifescape 則意味著廣義的環境，也就是人類生活的空間，包括精神、思想與感官可及的領域。

Yuyu Yang was born in Ilan in 1926. He dedicated his life in the conceptual sculpturing and aesthetics. His sculpture works, specially his stainless steel works, exhibit a harmonious relation between humanity and Mother Nature. As compared to the English word, landscape, which means certain images on land that may be actually seen or perceived, Mr. Yang promoted the concept of "lifescape" which covers the invisible, yet more profound, components like spirit and thoughts, as opposed to the human's superficially perceived images.

▲ 創作中的朱銘
This photo shows Ju Ming focusing on his work.

# The artist—Ju Ming

In 1976, Yuyu Yang gave Ju Ming an exhibition opportunity. Mr. Yang was scheduled to have an exhibit at the National Museum of History, however he wanted to give Ju Ming an opportunity so he arranged to have Mr. Ju's works shown instead. It was through this exhibition that Ju Ming became recognized as a real artist in Taiwan. At that time, the nativist culture was quite popular, and Ju Ming and Hong Tong were regarded as the most representative artists of the nativist movement. Though his works of Taichi Series in wood were in the exhibition, his other works depicting native themes, such as Buffalo, were the focus of the attention of the public.

It was Mr. Yang's suggestion that made Ju Ming start to learn taichi boxing. Because he was always quite concentrated in everything he did, he learned taichi boxing with the same mind set, which allowed him to obtain the essence and true meaning of the ancient boxing, which were then incorporated into his works. In the 1970s, his works were exhibited in different Asian countries, and his Taichi Series works established him as a great artist in Asia. To further his studies, he went to New York in 1981. He developed another sculpture series, Living World Series, in that distant city. His Living World Series—Painted Wood sculptures were put on display to the public in New York for the first time.

Later on, Living World Series works lead Ju Ming to experiment on a variety of materials. He tried to use foam rubber and ropes to make the original molds and then cast them in bronze which could still show the feeling of foam rubber's elasticity. Therefore, he used this method to make a multiple of sportsmen sculptures. From the mid 1980s, Ju Ming has been working on collages and sculptures in pottery, stone and stainless steel. All his works after his Taichi Series were classified as Living World Series because all of them were regarding humans. Ju Ming is a person of honesty and bravery. He has to carry out an idea or a belief once he decides to do so. As Mr. Yuyu Yang's expected, Ju Ming has established himself as a true artist in art history of Taiwan.

▼ 1997年於巴黎梵登廣場個展
Place Vendôme, Paris 1997

# Chronology

# 朱銘 年表

# 朱銘年表

| | |
|---|---|
| 1938 | 生於台灣苗栗通霄 |
| 1950 | 通霄國小畢業 |
| 1953-57 | 從李金川學木刻 |
| 1968-76 | 從楊英風學現代雕塑 |
| 1976 | 國立歷史博物館個展，台北 |
| 1977 | 東京中央美術館個展，東京 |
| 1978 | 東京中央美術館個展，東京 |
| 1979 | 春之藝廊個展，台北 |
| 1980 | 香港藝術中心個展，香港 |
| 1981 | 國立歷史博物館個展，台北 |
| —— | 漢查森藝廊個展，紐約 |
| 1983 | 漢查森藝廊個展，紐約 |
| 1984 | 艾雅拉博物館個展，馬尼拉 |
| —— | 比乃西現代美術館個展，曼谷 |
| 1985 | 漢查森藝廊個展，紐約 |
| 1986 | 交易廣場個展，香港 |
| —— | 新加坡歷史博物館個展，新加坡<br>（原新加坡國家博物館） |
| 1987 | 台北市立美術館個展，台北 |
| 1988 | 國立台灣美術館個展，台中<br>（原台灣省立美術館） |

# Chronology

| | |
|---|---|
| 1989 | 菲立斯・康達藝廊個展，紐約 |
| 1991 | 香港藝術中心個展，香港 |
| —— | 南岸中心個展，倫敦 |
| —— | 布朗斯與達比藝廊，倫敦 |
| —— | 約克夏雕塑公園個展，英國 |
| —— | 新光三越百貨公司個展，台北 |
| —— | 登克爾克現代美術館個展，法國 |
| 1992 | 台北漢雅軒個展，台北 |
| —— | NICAF國際藝術博覽會，橫濱 |
| —— | 台北市立美術館個展，台北 |
| —— | ART ASIA亞洲藝術博覽會，香港 |
| 1993 | 新宿三越百貨公司，東京 |
| 1994 | 榮嘉現代美術館，新竹 |
| 1995 | 箱根雕刻之森美術館回顧展，日本 |
| —— | ART ASIA亞洲藝術博覽會，香港 |
| 1997 | 巴黎梵登廣場個展，法國 |
| 1999 | 盧森堡市個展，盧森堡 |
| 1999 | 朱銘美術館開幕，台北 |
| 2000 | 布魯塞爾個展，比利時 |

| | |
|---|---|
| 1938 | Born at Miaoli of Tunghsiao, Taiwan |
| 1950 | Graduated from Tunghsiao Elementary School |
| 1953-57 | Apprenticeship with Master Lee Chin-chuan |
| 1968-76 | Began the training of modern sculpture with Yuyu Yang |
| 1976 | National Museum of History, Taipei |
| 1977 | Tokyo Central Museum, Tokyo |
| 1978 | Tokyo Central Museum, Tokyo |
| 1979 | Spring Gallery, Taipei |
| 1980 | Hong Kong Arts Centre, Hong Kong |
| 1981 | National Museum of History, Taipei |
| | Max Hutchinson Gallery, New York |
| 1983 | Max Hutchinson Gallery, New York |
| 1984 | Ayala Museum, Manila |
| | Bhirasri Institute of Modern Art, Bangkok |
| 1985 | Max Hutchinson Gallery, New York |
| 1986 | Exchange Square, Hong Kong |
| | Singapore History Museum, Singapore |
| 1987 | Taipei Fine Arts Museum, Taipei |
| 1988 | Taiwan Art Museum, Taichung, Taiwan |
| 1989 | Phyllis Kind Gallery, New York |
| 1991 | Hong Kong Arts Centre, Hong Kong |
| | South Bank Centre, London |
| | Browses & Darby Gallery, London |
| | Yorkshire Sculpture Park, U.K. |
| | Shin Kong Mitsukoshi Department Store Co, Ltd, Taipei |
| | Musée d'Art Contemporain de Dunkerque, France |
| 1992 | Hanart (Taipei) Gallery, Taipei |
| | NICAF YOKOHAMA'92, Japan |
| | Taipei Fine Arts Museum, Taipei |
| | ART ASIA—International Fine Art Expositions, Hong Kong |
| 1993 | Mitsukoshi Department Store in Shinjuku, Tokyo |
| 1994 | Glory Sculpture Park, Hsinchu, Taiwan |
| 1995 | Hakone Open-Air Museum, Japan |
| | ART ASIA—International Art Expositions, Hong Kong |
| 1997 | Place Vendôme, Paris |
| 1999 | Luxembourg City, Luxembourg |
| 1999 | Grand Opening of Juming Museum, Taipei |
| 2000 | Bruxelles, Belgium |

Collection of the Museum

館藏 精選

玩沙的女孩 | 1961，木，26x36x43 公分
A Girl Playing with Sand | 1961, Wood, 26x36x43 cm

刻畫出女孩神情專注，低頭在沙上畫著。創作的時候朱家夫婦還是新婚，朱銘很想在工藝製作外，另有真正出自自己意願的作品，特別央求太太抽空當模特兒，讓他刻製雕像。多年以後，朱銘帶著這件作品，敲開了楊英風家的大門，有妻子作見證，朱銘揮別雕刻匠的生涯，邁入另一段人生。

Here is a sculpture depicting a girl concentrating on playing with the sand. When Mr. Ju made this sculpture, he had just been married for a short while and he asked his wife to pose as the model because he wanted to create a sculpture coming from his heart. After many years he had finished this work, he brought this work with him to knock at the door of Yuyu Yang's house. Mr. Yang transformed Ju Ming into an artist from a craftsman.

朱家住在板橋江子翠的時候，附近有很多農田和糞坑，開放式的糞坑一經太陽曝曬，看起來就跟泥土地一樣。這天有個小朋友不小心掉進去，同伴都嚇跑了，只有朱家二女兒艷鵬拼了命，硬是把幾乎滅頂的朋友拉上來。朱銘特地為此情景創作一件木雕，楊英風老師聽說了雕像背後的故事，而將它命名為「小媽祖」。

When Ju Ming and his family lived at Panchiao in Taipei County, there was a lot of farmlands and cesspits in this area. Those open cesspits looked just like hardened earth after drying by the sun. One day, a child accidentally fell into a pit, the rest of children got scared and ran away from the scene except Mr. Ju's second daughter, Yen-peng, who bravely dragged up the child who almost drowned in the cesspit. Ju Ming made a sculpture to display the brave rescue. Yuyu Yang named the sculpture "The Little Matsu" after he heard the story behind the sculpture.

同心協力 | 1996，木，330x83x124 公分
In One Heart | 1996, Wood, 330x83x124 cm

描寫水牛拖運木料在坡道上前行，一旁有兩人奮力推車的景象。蔣勳對這件作品有很詳細的描述，「從後面推車一人的腳跟開始，向左邊上升到板車頂上堆得最高的一塊巨木的頂端，再向下斜降到因為用力而低垂得和地面接觸的牛頭，整個形成一道近於半圓的拋物線，拋物線隱含的實體是一個三角形，這是最能傳達『重壓感』的幾何形；朱銘因此使我們感覺到那巨木的重，那工作的負荷，然而這重，這負荷卻又因為在拋物線向前流動的暗示下，說服我們一定要相信，這些人、這牛，是有能力把這樣沉重的負荷、這樣艱鉅的工作推送上坡」。一九七六年展出的「同心協力」已為收藏家所收藏，美術館收藏的是朱銘以同一題材再創作的木雕。

One of Ju Ming's well-known works, In One Heart, made in 1976, was bought by a private collector after the first exhibition at the National Museum of History. The Juming Museum now displays the new one that Mr. Ju created in 1996 with the same subject. In One Heart depicts a buffalo dragging a cart full of logs upwards on a steep slope with two people pushing the cart on the sides. The art critic, Mr. Chiang Hsun, had a detailed description of the work: "The overall geometry of the work including the buffalo, whose head was almost touching the ground due to the heavy load, and the two men form a half of a parabola or a triangle, which vividly illustrates the heaviness of the load. Ju Ming wants us to feel the heaviness, and the configuration of half of a parabola can convince us that through teamwork the load will be pushed upward without doubt!"

太極系列—掰開太極 | 1971，木，38x37x43 公分
Taichi Series—Split Taichi | 1971, Wood, 38x37x43 cm

「太極系列」的作品並非是特地經營出的題材，而是在朱銘跟隨楊英風期間每日的健身活動，久而久之，他在其中領悟到太極的精神境界，直到滿腦子都是太極，乃至於萌生隨時都想雕刻太極的意念，由內而外，落實於身體與技法的結合。

廖仁義

Ju Ming did not plan on making the Taichi Series. After practicing taichi boxing every day while he was under the guidance of Yuyu Yang, he gradually understood the spiritual aspect of taichi boxing and his mind was filled with it. Therefore, he combined this spiritual aspect of taichi with his sculpture skill to create the Taichi Series works.

Jen-i Liao

太極系列—掰開太極 ｜ 1983，青銅，220x148x290 公分
Taichi Series—Split Taichi ｜ 1983, Bronze, 220x148x290 cm

朱銘從傳統雕像的寫實主義桎梏中解放自己，大刀闊斧地削掉無關宏旨的細節，讓最樸、最真的造型自然顯露出來。朱銘他並沒有放棄與木材的無間合作，相反的，他摸索到發洩精力的新途徑。他不再用鑿刀劈木，改用鏈鋸，並用曲柄鋸撕開木材，順著木材的紋理徒手劈、鑿、撕，使雕像的動態與姿勢凸顯出來，強化了表現力，這好比書法家以筆觸神奇地表現了方向、平衡、律動與力量。

蘇立文

Ju Ming liberated himself from the realism of his traditional figures, and learned to pare away unnecessary detail to reveal the essential form. But Ju Ming did not abandon the intense involvement with wood that was so natural to him. On the contrary, he found a new release for his energy in the way in which he fashioned his taichi figures. He abandoned the chisel for splitting the wood, using the chainsaw, tearing it open with a manual crank-spreader, hacking, gouging, ripping it apart with his bare hands, following the natural grain so that the figure's movements and gestures are intensified, become powerfully expressive in much the same way the brushstrokes of a master calligrapher express direction and balance, movement and energy.

Michael Sullivan

太極系列―單鞭下勢 | 1986，青銅，470x171x255 公分
Taichi Series—Single Whip | 1986, Bronze, 470x171x255 cm

太極作品可以說是朱銘壯年時代最受矚目的作品，在太極廣場中擺放的絕大部分太極的巨型銅雕，除了作品體積龐大之外，每件作品所展現的氣勢，也都使我們覺得彷彿置身於有無相生的太極境界之中。事實上，草根性一直涵藏於朱銘的生命深處，在他的雕塑生命中，他所關懷的是比草根性還要屬於藝術課題的精神性，特別是生命之中的精神性，而太極系列便是這個基本關懷的表現。
廖仁義

Ju Ming's Taichi Series, made in his middle age, is his most famous series. In the Taichi Square, most of the works on display are large-size bronze works cast from styrofoam molds. Besides their sheer size, the magnificent shapes and lines put visitors in the state of taichi. Although his grass root background and plain folk demeanor are the important attribute of him; throughout his sculpture career, what he has most concerned himself with has been the spiritual aspect, especially the spiritual aspect associated with life. His works of the Taichi Series are the tangible embodiment of his concern of the spiritual aspect.

Jen-i Liao

太極系列—十字手 | 1988，青銅，317x148x310 公分
Taichi Series—Preparation For Underarm Strike | 1988, Bronze, 317x148x310 cm

　英國藝評家房義安：「在朱銘的太極雕塑中，朱銘心手如一，創造了巨大的張力與戲劇性。而無論是從任何角度去看他的作品，這種張力與戲劇性都是持續不斷的。這些太極人物的無臉性與匿名性，允許我們從每一個各別的位置去面對他的作品，而倘若朱銘刻意去進行細部處理，以使每件作品呈現個體化的人格特徵，那麼這種面對作品的方式反而會變得不可能了。」

The British art critic, Ian Findlay, commented on Ju Ming's works: "In Ju Ming's Taichi Series works, each of them possesses tremendous amount of tension and astonishment, which exist at any angle of a work. Also, all of them are faceless and unidentifiable; however, if Ju Ming had altered these characteristics of his works, his works would be much less attractive and not so intriguing!"

朱銘的大刀闊斧在作品中呈現出來的人體造型，正好跟現代雕塑的抽象理念不謀而合。「太極系列」的每件作品，都流露出抽象的運動性，非但不受限於太極拳分解圖的運動公式，甚至還改造了我們對運動空間認知習慣，讓作品與空間的關係都抽象了起來；特別是當這種抽象關係發生之後，我們發現，每件作品都允許我們從不同的視點去看，而且各個視點下的塊面也都能夠根據作品整體，處於有機的呼應關係之中。　　廖仁義

The lines and forms of Ju Ming's works meet those of the abstract concept of modern sculpture. Each of his works displays an abstract motion, not confined by the movements of the taichi boxing. Taichi Series changes our perception of motion and space, and hence makes the relationship between the works and space abstract. With this unique relationship, each of his works may be viewed from a different angle and a different perception will be obtained by the viewers.

Jen-i Lioa

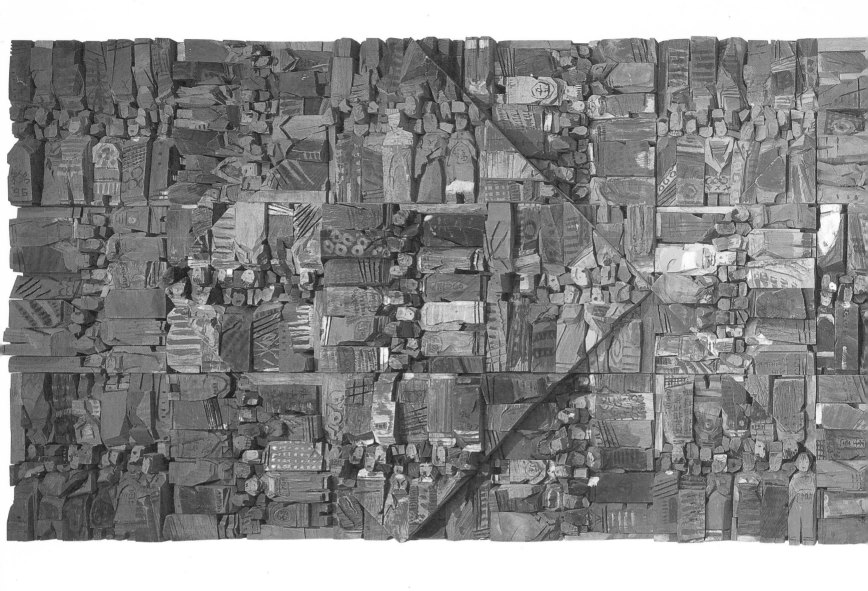

人間系列 | 1995~1996，木，847x27x231 公分
Living World Series | 1995~1996, Wood, 847x27x231 cm

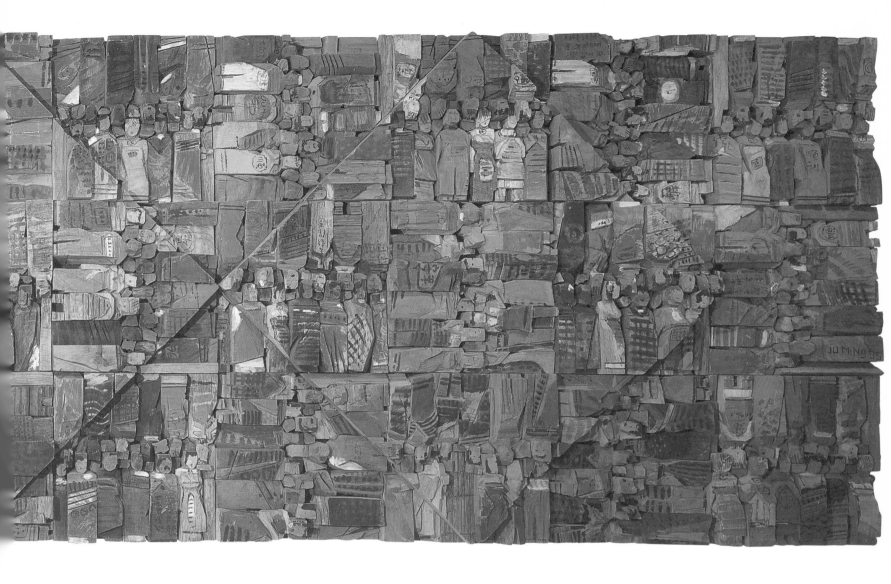

從八十年代開始，朱銘的「人間系列」問世。木刻的、不銹鋼板撬折的，大大小小，扶老攜幼；朱銘的「人間」已經成了小宇宙。他自己說的：「人間系列乃是人間百態的抽樣表達」，而這個主題透過了好幾種不同的材質來表達：有海綿翻銅、活潑粗獷的銅人間；有嚴峻典雅由不銹鋼板撬曲捲折的不銹鋼系列；還有溫和喜悅，親切而艷麗的彩木系列。　　　張頌仁

Ju Ming's Living World Series first appeared in the early 1980s as a collection of wood sculpture. Since then, he has enriched this theme with works in ceramics, in bronze-cast bundled foam rubber and in crushed stainless steel sheets. These figures are portrayed in various age groups and walks of life, both at work and at play. In time, the Living World Series has grown into a veritable world of people. In Ju Ming's own words, it is a choice "sampling" of the rich diversity of humanity.

Chang Tsong-zung

( Johnson Chang )

人間系列 | 1995～1996，木，等身
Living World Series | 1995～1996, Wood, life size

彩繪木雕洋溢著市井人家的生活氣息，在展覽廳內兩兩三三地私
語或失神地凝想。他們看來都似乎熟悉，但又充滿神秘，像日常
可見的人，他們忙著自己的日常事務，可是觀眾又無法瞭解這些
人心中的世界。「彩繪木雕」是朱銘表達他對現代人世風貌的作
品，這些作品充滿時代氣息，是屬於今天的文化。「人間」系列
的不斷推陳出新，表現了朱銘旺盛的創作力，並代表了現代中國
藝術在國際藝壇的份量。　　　　　　　　　　　　　　張頌仁

These colorful wood figures articulate the vitality of our daily life. Even
when grouped together in exhibition, they seem to continue their endless
gossip and intimate gestural exchanges. To the viewers, the Living
World figures are both familiar and strange, for they are people whom
we all seem to know, and yet the closed world of their personal concerns
is forever sealed from us. Ju Ming believes there is no need for us to
know their private affairs; neither do we need to read their minds. They
are simply people who cohabit the world with us, with whom we share a
living community. The Living World Series is Ju Ming's personal
expression of his sentiments about our world. It is contemporary in
spirit and full of vitality. The rich creative possibility Ju Ming brings to
demonstrates his power as an artist, and establishes him as a leading
sculptor of our time.　　　　　　　　　　　　Chang Tsong-zung
（Johnson Chang）

人間系列—降落傘　　1987～1988，青銅、不銹鋼，等身
Living World Series—Parachute　　1987～1988, Bronze, Stainless steel, life size

這件作品曾於一九九一年十二月應法國西北部登克爾克市的當代
藝術館之邀展出，也是主辦單位當時的指定作品。在材料上，降
落傘是以不銹鋼及銅作成的，跳傘者則是海綿翻銅。不銹鋼雖堅
硬，卻由於閃爍的光澤而給人隨風鼓動的印象，而海綿翻銅所傳
達的彈性觸感，又還原了人體一種敏捷的機動性。　　　廖仁義

This work, Parachute, one of Ju Ming's Living World Series was once
exhibited at Musée d'Art Contemporain de Dunkerque in France in
December of 1991. The parachute was made of stainless steel and
bronze, which gives a sensation of motion in the sky because of their
shimmering reflection. The original mold of the human figure was made
of foam rubber and then cast in bronze. The foam rubber imparted to the
figure a realistic agility because of its elasticity.　　　Jen-i Liao

人間系列 | 1987，青銅，179x136x173 公分
Living World Series | 1987, Bronze, 179x136x173 cm

人間系列 | 1987，青銅，90x195x220 公分
Living World Series | 1987, Bronze, 90x195x220 cm

這些以撐竿跳，跨欄、體操、吊單槓、摩托車為題材的運動作品中，每一件作品雖然都是運動過程的一個分解動作，但是我們可以從身體的內在運動感覺中發現，它們都表現出承先啟後的動作連續性。因為，我們的視線並不是呆滯地框限於眼前作品的物質性現實之中，而是從作品中運動身體的活動支點出發，跟隨著身體的律動方向在游動；至於我們的記憶感覺與預期，也都伴隨著這個動勢而層層交疊地銜接起來。 廖仁義

These works of Living World Series illustrate the sports of pole-vaulting, hurdling, gymnastics, horizontal bar and motorcycling. Though each work depicts only a frame in the continuous motion, it still shows its close relationship to the whole range of motion. Through these works, we can picture the continuity and beauty of the sports. Because our unlimited vision is responding automatically to the rhythm of our body movements from dynamic leverage, our perception and expectation integrate the illusory athletic movements at the same time.

Jen-i Liao

人間系列 | 1987，青銅，（左）178x117x270 公分，（中）179x136x173 公分，（右）180x140x195 公分
Living World Series | 1987, Bronze, ( L ) 178x117x270 cm, ( M ) 179x136x173 cm, ( R ) 180x140x195 cm

41

人間系列 ｜ 1987，青銅，（左)95x100x133 公分，（中)65x143x148 公分，（右)73x50x170 公分
Living World Series ｜ 1987, Bronze, ( L )95x100x133 cm, ( M )65x143x148 cm, ( R )73x50x170 cm

在人間系列與人等身大的作品中，朱銘利用海綿及保麗龍鑄銅，被捆著的人像型態扭曲，沒有面容但表情氣鼓鼓的，呈現一股詼諧、活潑、豪放、野性的味道。若非這些作品蘊蓄著的力量飽和得幾欲掙脫綑綁身上的皮帶子，我們也許會不經意地視他們為消遣之作。雖然「人間」與「太極」意蘊、風格迥異，它們卻都分享了朱銘那份使造型生活化的天賦異稟。　　　　　蘇立文

The works of Living World Series in life size or larger consist of bloated, faceless pneumatic figures in contorted attitudes made from wrapped and folded styrofoam bound with thongs and cast in bronze–comic, lively, liberated, outrageous. If these figures were not packed with a power so great that they almost burst the ropes that bind them, we would dismiss them as pure fun. Although they are utterly different in spirit from the taichi figures, they shared Ju Ming's extraordinary gift for investing form with life.

Michael Sullivan

人間系列　｜ 1993，不銹鋼，267x125x161 公分
Living World Series ｜ 1993, Stainless steel, 267x125x161 cm

以不銹鋼為媒材所創作的人間系列作品中，朱銘以簡潔熟練的抽象形式演繹其眼底下的眾生百態。朱銘偶爾也會被捆在人物造像的探索和人類心靈孤寂的困境中，不過努力的探索，使他成為一個貫徹到底的台灣雕塑家。每一個新系列的誕生，皆意味著他向創作里程邁進一步，而每一個新造像就彰顯他的新理念和頓悟。朱銘的作品在台灣當代雕塑家中最為簡潔直接，不單只因為雕塑家取材於現成的環境，更在於他以精猛、原始的動力與鮮有的率性去正視創作者的角色。　　　　　　　　　房義安

The Living World Series in stainless steel is Ju Ming's most austere and calculatingly abstract interpretation of his view of the human figure. Though Ju Ming sometimes seems to be trapped in a narrow exploration of the human figure and the human predicament of being alone, his searching makes him out as one of the most consistent of Taiwanese sculptors. Each new series created is a step forward in an endless journey of discovery. Each figure he created is another part of his perception and understanding that both enlightens and refreshes. That his work is the most instantly recognizable of Taiwan's main contemporary sculptors is not simply because his theme is a ready one, but because he confronts his role of creator with a raw emotion and high energy as well as a sense of candor that is unusually direct.

Ian Findlay

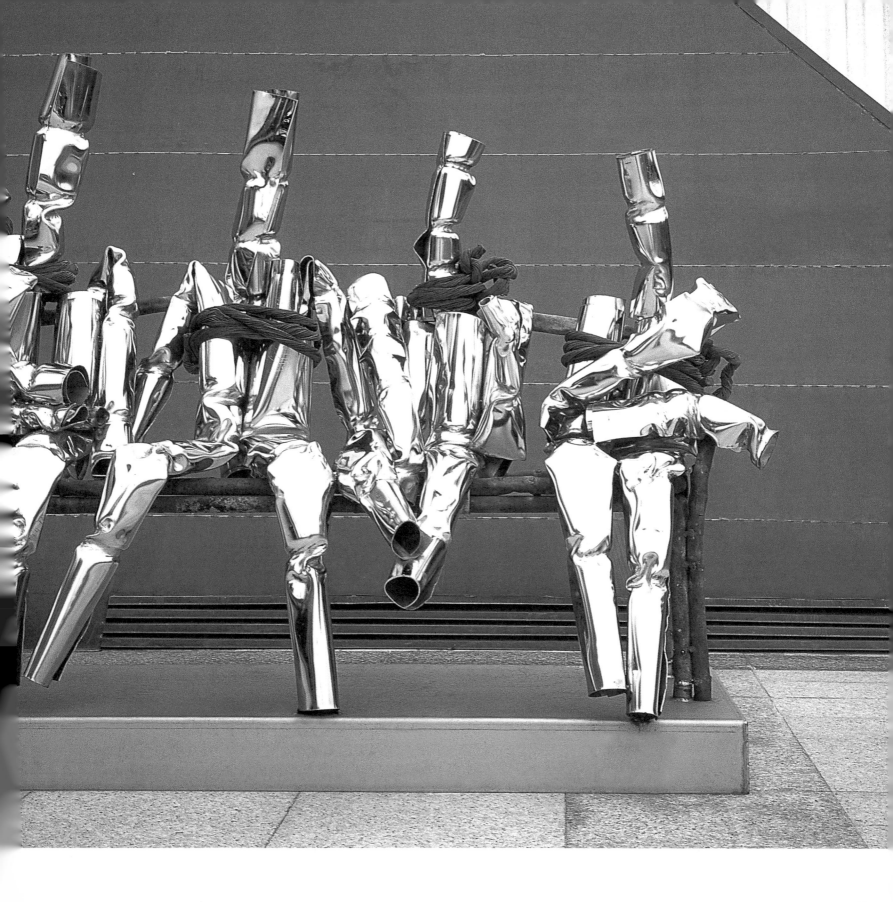

人間系列 | 1990，瓷土，（左）14x12x40 公分，（右）14x15x34 公分
Living World Series | 1990, Porcelain, ( L )14x12x40 cm, ( R )14x15x34 cm

除了新題材和新材料，朱銘另一個演變在於新的製作方式，新的作業情態。陶塑人物和群魚最明顯：人物的外衣亦是他們的軀體，同時又意味了他們的神氣和骨架。陶魚雖然寫實，但並不是超寫實地逼真，可是其神態的真實感已叫朱銘家中的小貓垂涎大嚷。朱銘創造的神似與活生物互相的確有靈犀一點通處。

司考特　洛伊

Ju Ming has become comfortable with change not only in the new media but also in the ways he treats his subjects. The ceramic figure and ceramic fish could be the good representative. Looking at the figures the inside and the outside at the same time. The outsides of the robes on the figures are also the bodies and each has the feeling of yet a specific body structure and skeleton. The ceramic fish is not photo real but real enough in character-essence to tease Ju Ming's cats into howling fits when the fish were hanging up outside his house. Living things relate to the "living" things Ju Ming creates.

R. Scott Lloyd

朱銘用了身邊隨手可得的材料—碎布、衣服、選舉旗幟、標語、報紙等，並在上面加上人物的速寫甚至是文字註解，每個物件似乎都在訴說著不同的故事、表達著各樣的情感，材料與材料之間互相對話。人間系列中各種媒材的應用就如同他所強調，「我們尊重材料並非利用材料，而尊重材料也不能受它限制創作的主題。」

Ju Ming sketches and writes on common objects like cloth pieces, clothing, election banners, slogans, newspapers, etc., so each item seems to tell a different story, sending a variety of feelings. Ju Ming had the following comment on the fact that he used various materials and items in his Living World Series: "Respecting materials has nothing to do with utilizing them in the best way. And again, the subject of a work should never be constrained or restricted by such materials used."

人間系列 | 1998，墨，24.5x33 公分
Living World Series | 1998, Ink, 24.5x33 cm

朱銘在一次接受訪問時說到「我的個性不願意重複，喜歡變新。」所以在「人間系列」中他挑戰不同的媒材創作，在嘗試了一段時間的陶塑之後，開始創作平面式的作品，他以水墨為線條，使用鮮豔的色彩畫魚、雞、蔬果和人物，其實他所畫的就是他「人間系列」雕刻的素描加彩，明亮的色彩加上恣意豪放的線條，這是雕刻家的繪畫，很顯然他的雕塑與繪畫是合而為一的。

Ju Ming once stated in an interview, "I do not like to repeat what I did before. I like variations and doing different things." After he finished a few works in his Living World Series, he started to do plane paintings. He used bright colors and traditional Chinese brush to paint fish, chicken, vegetables, people and his Living World Series. With free flowing lines, these paintings illustrate how a sculptor incorporated his sculpturing technique and sculptures into his paintings.

# 觀朱雋的石頭世界

梅丁衍

詩曰：混沌未分天地亂，茫茫渺渺無人見。自從盤古破鴻蒙，門關從茲清濁辨。

詩經上又有記載：宇宙由混沌而後始有根，地始凝結；然後重濁下凝，有山、有石、有土、有人有禽獸。至此，人與大自然發生了密切的生態關係。早在石器時代，人類祖先就已懂得把石頭當作求生必備的工具，石頭成為記錄人類文明歷史的里程碑。石頭的種類，雖然良莠不齊，但是畢竟玉不琢磨不成器，石不雕不成材，也只有透過藝術家的匠心獨運之功，一塊平凡無奇的石頭才可能成為人類的珍寵。

朱雋就是秉持這樣一個平易想法，走入他的石頭世界。由於台灣特殊的地質結構，溪谷石成為最廣見的河床景觀，大片光禿圓滾的石群，赤裸裸的曝曬在烈日狂雨之下，其頑靈不亢的性格，激發了朱雋對萬物有情的領悟，或許這些堅實粗糙石頭的內在，未必盡是鐵石心腸！在一次偶然機會中，朱雋看到一塊自然崩裂的石頭，這塊石頭呈現有如鋸齒般的裂紋，在群石當中，他是那麼的突兀孤憐，於是朱雋想到治癒這個傷口，就像外科手術師一樣，他小心翼翼的進行縫合工作，不同的是，朱雋在這塊石頭的裂痕處裝上了銅製的拉鍊，手術雖告完成，拉鍊也已裝置，但是傷痕依然存在，原來石頭依然是石頭，風化後崩裂的石頭，其實已經暗示了自身的宿命，任何治癒工程為時已晚。也許，真正的療效，恐怕只有再次回歸於自然界的風雨洗禮吧！但是，對朱雋而言，治癒只能算是一種意念，是一種與自然界對話的態勢，裝上拉鍊的石頭，就好比生態學者把採拾來的生物，經過實驗室的標本手續，最後附予銘誌，陳列在博物館內，供人觀賞。這些「選物」是註定享有人類特殊關照的。

在傳統的雕塑技巧中，「雕」是減法，「塑」則是加法；而在雕塑的空間概念裡，則是虛與實，陰與陽的二元互補存有關係。但是，朱雋的石頭上裝上了拉鍊，則既不屬於「雕」，也不屬於「塑」，他是一種空間觀念臨界面的探討，就好比門扉的意義，它可以是開啟的，也可以是關閉的，在概念上，他是空間存有的暗示訊碼，如果沒有門，兩種空間就無法產生對話。因此，石頭上的拉鍊與石頭本身，形成了有如詩作般的超現實體，這種稍微動動手腳，就可以改變事物內涵的「並置」手法，便是「點石成金」的最佳寫照，一些裝上拉鍊的石頭，有的形似荷包，酷似飽滿的綿墊，而拉鍊本身的柔軟度與啟動功能，使得石頭堅硬的質感一再癱瘓，這是朱雋令「頑石點頭」的另一寫照。

在中國歷史神話故事裡，有不少傳奇人物都與石頭有關，相傳夏禹的兒子啟，就是石頭轉世，而西遊記裡的孫悟空則是由仙石風化而成，觀看朱雋的石頭，的確予人一種「靈根育孕離流出，心性修持大道生」的期許。

# Observing the Stone World of Ju Jun

Before it grew out of the void, the world was a murky, uninhabited mass. Once Pan Gu separated heaven and earth, the divide between the clear and the unclear became visible.

The Book of Odes says that only after the primeval state of the universe ended did the heavens find a point to rest upon and the earth begin to take shape, after which the "myriad things," such as mountains, stones, soil, humans, and animals followed. At this time, man and nature became tied together in an intimate ecological relationship. As far back as the Stone Age, early man knew how to make use of stones as essential implements of survival, thus stones became a milestone in the recorded history of civilization. While great variation exists between different kinds of stones, it is human carving which really sets them apart, as only the creative touch of an artist can transform an ordinary stone into a marvel of civilization.

It is such an unassuming approach that Ju Jun carried into his world of stones. Given Taiwan's unusual geological structure, creek stones are a common sight: broad creek beds are covered with round stones, exposed before the sun and the trenchant rains. Their resolute nature awakened Ju Jun's sense of the spiritual nature of the "myriad things" of creation that maybe behind their tough exteriors lie feeling hearts. On one occasion Ju Jun happened upon a stone that had split naturally in such a way as to reveal tooth-like markings, as if it had been cut with a saw. Struck by the way this particular stone stood out from the rest of its brethrens; Ju Jun was moved to try to "heal" its "wound". And so, he cautiously set about stitching it up as a surgeon figure. Unlike the commom surgeon, Ju Jun affixed a copper zipper on the opening. While the special operation was completed with the installation of a zipper, the wound remained, demonstrating that a stone split by the elements has begun to give in to its fate—any remedial operations are too late. Then again, perhaps the most significant effect on such an operation is that the stone fears it will be reborn to face the heartless assault of the elements once again. But for Ju Jun, "treatment" is merely an impulse, or a means of communion with nature. Stones on which zippers have been installed are somewhat like life specimens collected by ecologists. After being subjected to experimentation, are assigned names and codes and displayed in museums for the public. These specimens are unique because they are destined to receive special attention from human being.

In traditional sculpture technique, engraving or carving are like subtraction, and molding or shaping are like addition. Such an arithmetical concept of space is founded on the complementary relationship of opposites. However, Ju Jun's attachment of zippers to stones is, strictly speaking, neither carving or shaping, addition or subtraction, but rather an exploration of the concept of the critical territory of space—like a door, it can be open or closed. Conceptually, it is a signifier of the existence of space, as dialogue would be impossible between the two kinds of spaces without a door. Thus the zipper and the stone together, like a poem, become a surreal entity. This kind of juxtaposition, where in the essence of objects can be altered with just a few actions, is a perfect illustration of the Midas-like transformation of rocks into gold. Some zipper-wearing stones look like wallets, others may appear as plump pillows, while the pliability of the zippers and their ability to be opened soften the solid, rough texture of the stones. This is where Ju Jun succeeds brilliantly in getting stones to comply with his aspirations.

Mei Dean-e

朱雋館 | 1993～1994，青銅、不銹鋼，981x560x1150 公分
Ju Jun Area | 1993～1994, Bronze, Stainless steel, 981x560x1150 cm

| 石頭與拉鍊 | 1997，青銅、水泥，2260x2800x32 公分 |
|---|---|
| Stone & Zipper | 1997, Bronze, Cement, 2260x2800x32 cm |

| 石頭與拉鍊 | 1997，青銅、石，190x144x137 公分 |
|---|---|
| Stone & Zipper | 1997, Bronze, Stone, 190x144x137 cm |

虛實之間—朱雋和「拉鍊系列」雕塑。

在這個系列裡，巨型拉鍊被裝置在不同的材質上，有的拉開地表露出一池荷花，還有拉開不銹鋼帳蓬和大石頭的拉鍊，這個可開可關的用具，引發觀眾想一探究竟的好奇心，也讓原本堅硬的材質變得柔軟起來；拉鍊原本具有保護、防禦、可開放的性質，當它被運用到石頭上時，隱隱成為「門」的象徵，充滿著想跨越、想穿透甚至想一探究竟的故事情境。

In Ju Jun's Zipper Series works, giant zippers are placed on different items: some works including a pond of lotuses, stainless steel tent and large stone that may be seen by undoing a large zipper. The zipper design induces the curiosity of the people and in some way softens the hard texture of the enclosed steel and stone. Zipper itself possesses the functions or characteristics of protection, enclosure and accessibility. When a large zipper is used in Ju Jun's work to enclose an item, the zipper metaphorically represents a door or gateway, inducing a desire to look at the content.

畢 卡索，巴布羅 路易茲，1881年生於西班牙的馬拉加（Malaga）。父親為藝術教師，他第一個繪畫老師就是他的父親，就因為畢卡索有這樣好的一個家庭，他繪畫天才獲得了良好的培養。

一九○○年初至巴黎，是他繪畫的「藍色時期」（Blue Period)，當時他的作品受到一些畫都市生活的法國畫家，如孟克（Munch）和土魯茲－羅特列克（Toulouse-Lautrec）等人的影響。一九○五年進入「玫瑰色時期」（Rose Period)，此時他的生活比較愉快，畫面也明亮起來，畫面上的主題常出現江湖上的賣藝人，而這時期也開始奠定了畢卡索的藝術地位。

一九○七年開始漸漸脫離了寫實的風格，並受非洲黑人雕刻的影響，接著進入另一個關鍵性的轉變，即分析立體主義的形成。首先破壞自然的物形，僅用線條結合成部份的畫面，然後再重新構成立體，也就是借重幾何的三角或四角的圖形，根據明暗的配置進行神秘的組合，畢卡索和布拉克(Braque)可說是「立體派」(Cubism)的倡導人。

一九一二年他發展出「拼貼」（Collage)，利用木片、鐵絲、紙、線條重新構成，他開啟了這個方向，但是並未繼續下去。一九一七年之後，由於接觸了古代美術與羅馬古典主義，開始繪製一系列紀念碑性的裸婦素描與油畫，到一九二三年後，開始將形體歪曲變形，之後更將人物解體，運用書法般的線條。

一九三○年代初期畢卡索開始以強烈的形式和耀眼的色彩繪製一系列裸像，隨後又展開一系列鬥牛作品，其中以格爾尼卡(Guernica)為代表。畢卡索的晚年仍然有創意、積極，他一生經歷豐富，集合了才華、機緣、長壽再加上他不斷精練的創作，成為二十世紀偉大的藝術家實在當之無愧。

Pablo Ruiz Picasso was born in Malaga, Spain in 1881. His father was an art teacher and the first painting teacher to Picasso. With the aid of his father, his talent in painting could be properly cultivated and developed from an early age.

In the early 1900s, Picasso moved to Paris and started his Blue Period. In that period, his works were influenced by a few urban-dwelling painters including Munch and Toulouse-Lautrec.

In 1905, he entered his Rose Period. In this period, he had a happier life and his palette began to lighten, bringing in a "rose" tone. His paintings were inundated by circus performers and clowns, and he gradually became a recognized and prestigious painter.

In 1907, affected by African sculpture techniques, Picasso developed Cubism, which was an important breakaway from the limited mimetic representation. Cubism was jointly developed by Picasso and Braque. Cubism was used more as a method of visually laying out the three-dimensional conceptual image of an object, as opposed to a perceptual one.

In 1912, Picasso developed collages, which incorporated actual objects including wood pieces, wires, paper, etc. into his works. However, after a few years, he turned away from the collages.

After he got in touch with classical fine arts and classical Roman arts, he started to draw a series of sketches and oil paintings of naked women. After 1923, his works showed dissected forms and shapes of figures.

In the early 1930s, Picasso started to paint a series of naked figures with conspicuous forms and bright colors; afterwards, he began to paint a series of works depicting bullfights (represented by Guernica).

In his senior years, he was still active in his paintings and full of creativity. With his unmatched talent, longevity and spirit of constant excelling, Picasso was indeed one of the greatest artists of the 20th century!

小丑 | 1966，油畫，65x90 公分
Clown | 1966, Oil on canvas, 65x90 cm

畢費，一九二八年生於法國，十五歲進入巴黎美術學校就讀，一九四六年首度舉行個展，兩年後獲法國的評論大獎。

二十歲的畢費，就已經聲名大噪，成了富翁。藝評在一九五五年將他評為戰後法國十大繪畫名家之一，法國還曾以他的作品發行郵票。畢費在海外受到推崇，但法國當代藝壇卻常抨擊他的作品。

畢費的畫作以鋸齒狀的線條和冷峻的色調聞名，他曾說，繪畫的主旨不在於取悅世人。因此畢費的作品中常見悲劇主題，灰暗的人物或戰亂的描寫。

他描寫戰後人心空虛、憤怒的作品，並運用了中古世紀哥德教堂中彩色玻璃的黑色輪廓線條，這些有力的線條表現了量感與速度，也擴張了整個畫面的張力，而色彩在相較下成了次要的元素。

畢費雖在國外享有盛名，但他最在意的還是法國藝壇不能接受他，而晚年受帕金森氏症的折磨，使藝術家無法繼續作畫，也讓他一度向友人表示厭世。一九九九年十月四日，畢費在法國東南的寓所自殺身亡，享年七十一歲。

Bernard Buffet was born in France in 1928. When he was 15, he started to study at the École des Beaux-Arts. In 1946 he had his first exhibition. In 1948, he was one of the two winners selected by Prix de la Critique.

He gained prestige and fortune when he was only 20. In 1955, he was recognized as one of the 10 most outstanding painters in France after WWII. His paintings were used on stamps in France. Though he received a lot of prestige from the overseas, he was constantly under attack from the artistic circles in France.

Many of his works were full of angular figures and mostly somber colors. He once said that he did not paint to please his viewers and the general public. Buffet favored tragic subjects, underdogs and horrors of war. His success lay in his synthesis of the thick, dark lines, which could express strength and speed, with the traditional techniques.

Though he was quite popular overseas, his biggest regret was the fact that the arts community circles in France could not accept him. In his senior years, he was tormented by Parkinson's disease. The disease crippled his ability to work. He once indicated to his friend that he wanted to die. On October 1999, he took his own life in his residence in France at the age of 71.

毛澤東 | 1972，絹印，( 91x91 公分 )×9
Mao Tse-tung | 1972, Silkscreen, ( 91x91 cm )×9

安迪 沃荷，一九二八年出生於賓夕法尼亞州匹茲堡的勞工家庭，原名是安德魯 沃荷。父母親是來自捷克的移民，其父原為營建工人，後改做採煤礦工，在一九四二年便去世了，其母以製作手工藝品掙取收入。沃荷在卡內基學院讀繪畫和設計，於一九四九年取得學士學位後，馬上前往紐約，從事插畫及商業繪畫生涯。

　　一九五〇年晚期他經常有展出，作品大多是從他商業插畫取材而來，引起的迴響並不大，但是這些商業藝術作品可說是普普藝術的序曲。因為普普藝術方面的成就，使他得以進入藝術史之中。一九六〇年代早期開始脫離商業藝術，轉而使用日常生活中隨處可得的圖像與物體來作為創作題材。他的工作室中每日所食用的午餐康寶湯罐和可口可樂促發了沃荷將之繪在畫布上的靈感。沃荷整個藝術生涯，為嚴謹的繪畫注入了許多豐富、令人議論卻又看似短暫如雲煙的題材。

　　從展示的廣告、漫畫、新聞相片到廣告劇照，在過程上，他如同是一位美國人生活方式的圖像紀錄者，將他那時代所展示過的人、產品和事件忠實地記錄下來，雖然他曾未宣傳過他藝術作品有任何偉大的精神，但他知道，他的作品忠實地反映了美國夢，並將美國夢加以美學上地創造。

Andy Warhol was born in Pittsburgh of Pennsylvania in 1928. He was given the name of Andrew Warhola at birth. His parents were immigrants from Czechoslovakia. His father was a construction worker and later became a coal miner. After his father died in 1942, his mother had to do craft work to support the family. He studied painting and design at the Carnegie Institute. After he got his college degree in 1949, he immediately went to New York and worked as a commercial painter.

In the late 1950s, his commercial works were put on exhibition on a constant basis. Though the exhibitions did not capture much attention, they were the prelude to his fame. His commercial works made him a member of pop artists.

In the early 1960s, he started to break away from the commercial art and used everyday life items and objects as motif of his work. For example, he drew many paintings on Campbell's soup cans and Coke bottles which he ate or drank at his studio.

Throughout his art career, he injected many rich yet controversial subjects into his paintings in ads, comics, photos, etc. Though he did not pass down any outstanding teaching, he faithfully recorded and displayed the American life in his era and his works truly reflected the American way and American dream through his unique aesthetic input.

斜臥人雕像 ｜ 1983，青銅，89x33x43 公分
Reclining Figure ｜ 1983, Bronze, 89x33x43 cm

習作 | 1958，墨水、蠟筆、紙，33x40 公分
Studies for Sculpture | 1958, Ink, Cray on Paper, 33x40 cm

亨利摩爾，一八九八年生於英國約克夏郡的卡斯佛 (Castleford)，父母親都是個性堅毅而善解人意，摩爾的童年生活相當快樂。一九二一年榮獲倫敦皇家藝術學院的獎學金，他善盡利用所有倫敦可能提供的資源與機會，定期參觀美術館，在那裡他對原始藝術產生了極大的興趣。

Henry Moore was born in Castleford, Yorkshire of the Great Britain, in 1898. Both his parents were quite caring and understanding and hence he had a very happy childhood. In 1921, he received a scholarship from the London Art College. After he went to see the art exhibitions in the museum on a constant basis, he developed a tremendous interest in the sculpture techniques.

亨利摩爾的藝術旅程中，其作品受早期英國中世紀雕塑的影響，爾後又對古埃及、希臘、文藝復興及早期墨西哥藝術產生極大興趣，而所有這些古拙風格，在他的一些作品中表現極為明顯，一種深厚穩重的形塊充滿了生命力。早在一九三○年代，摩爾便已成為英國藝術界裡一個相當重要的人物。

In his early period, his works were very much affected by the medieval British sculpture techniques. Later, he became strongly influenced by the art of ancient Egypt, Greece, the Renaissance and ancient Mexico. His works showed the tremendous impacts from these arts and his sculptures were full of vigor and vitality. He had already become a very important sculptor in Britain in the early 1930s.

亨利摩爾的整個創作事業生涯裡，一開始就固結於兩個主題〝斜躺的女人〞和〝母與子〞，這並不是蓄意的考慮，而是從某種內在之衝力的結果。某種來自潛意識的驅策力，從一九二○年代起他製作的雕像約有250件以上〝斜躺的女人〞。從一九二二到一九四○年，都是以〝母與子〞為主題，整體說來摩爾的雕塑作品呈現一種佔據性的空間量感與量塊間之肌理的表面張力及穿透的形式表現。

Throughout his artistic career, all his works revolved around two main themes: reclining figure and mother & child. The reason for this was that these two subjects were the greatest driving forces in his inner self or even subconscious, urging him to put these ideas into his sculptures. He did over 250 pieces of sculptures of reclining figures since 1920. From 1922 to 1940, all his works revolved around the mother & child. In an overview, his sculptures had the characteristics and form of a unique spatial links and abstract and a sense of penetration.

## Panoramic View

漫遊 美術館

JUMING MUSEUM

「服務中心」內設有藝術商品街與美食餐廳。藝術商品街提供了各式各樣與朱銘有關的商品及複製品；美食餐廳，則提供佳餚美食、點心與各式飲品，參觀者在欣賞藝術作品之餘，也能夠悠閒地用餐與購物。

「展覽室」為一棟兩層樓的室內展覽空間。除了館內典藏常設展外，也展出國內外著名藝術家作品。展覽室外則陳列朱銘「人間系列」與運動有關的作品，此處一件大型的降落傘曾於一九九一年在法國登克爾克美術館展出。

「會議室」是一處可以容內三百人的多功能會議空間，提供各界人士在一個優雅的藝術環境裡舉辦大型演講、研討會與員工訓練活動。會議室內的另一空間，則陳列著曾經陪伴朱銘美術館走過披荊斬棘艱苦歲月的兩部怪手，在它們退役下來以後，朱銘將它們重新整理並加上人物，成為他「人間系列」作品之一，為它們增添了生動的色彩。

「藝術表演區」為一個露天的表演活動場所。觀眾席則是參考古馬羅競技場拾級而上的弧形石階。美術館會不定期舉辦表演活動，也提供給相關表演團體演出。在藝術表演區的四周，為增添參觀者的藝術想像與趣味，朱銘放置了許多「人間系列」以不銹鋼、青銅創作而成的作品，這些作品也成為這個表演區的基本觀眾。

「朱雋館」朱雋是朱銘的長子，同時也是國內頗負盛名的雕塑家，近期所創作的〈拉鍊系列〉尤其突出。園區內可以看到主要三種類型作品，分別是大型新月型拉鍊荷花池、拉鍊帳蓬與拉鍊石頭。

「戲水區」整個戲水區包括了「許願池」、「蓮花池」、「戲水池」三種不同造景。「許願池」的周圍放置了朱銘〈人間系列〉石雕作品，朱銘說，這個構想類似義大利羅馬的許願池，這一尊尊石雕作品，彷彿正在俯瞰著人間，也同時身在人間呢！「蓮花池」則於每年夏季便會怒放著一片花海；「戲水池」就是開放給參觀者親近、嬉戲的淺水區。

「太極廣場」在綠草如茵的太極廣場上，共陳列了三十餘件

「太極系列」作品。此處所擺放的大部分是太極系列巨型保麗龍翻銅作品；除了作品體積龐大之外，每件作品所展現的氣勢，也都在在使我們覺得彷彿置身於有無相生的太極境界之中。

「美術館本館」本館建築的外觀為金字塔般的造型，最令人印象深刻的則為建築物的外體，是以不銹鋼與銅為主；館內陳列以朱銘早期木雕作品、彩繪木雕及平面作品為主。再者，館內還特別規劃兩間的展覽專室，紀念朱銘的兩位恩師—李金川及楊英風，他們兩位老師曾經先後給予朱銘在創作上不同而關鍵性的影響。

「人間廣場」從「太極廣場」走向「人間廣場」必須經過一座橋，這座橋便是朱銘為了紀念先母王愛女士而命名為「愛橋」。「人間廣場」上陳列的是「人間系列」作品，主要以青銅、海綿翻銅與石材作品為主，其中以「紳士」與「人間百態」兩件作品為主軸，專注刻畫描寫云云眾生的人間百態。

「藝術交流區」這是一處提供給專業藝術創作者發表作品的戶外廣場，透過美術館邀請或藝術家申請的方式展出。在漫遊遼闊的雕塑園區之際，除了欣賞朱銘的作品外，也能與當代藝術家傑出的創作進行交流、對話。

「慈母碑」是整個園區最早完工的地方。朱銘的作品中可以常見到母子情深的題材，慈母碑正是描寫朱銘對已逝母親的孺慕之情，也正是「人間系列」作品中探討親情關係的最佳表現；而圍繞在母親身邊或嬉戲或酣睡的正是朱銘與兄姐們。

「天鵝池」此區專門規劃作為一處給遊客休憩與閒談的空間；這座天鵝池畔，陳列著多件朱銘早期鄉土系列及較小型的太極系列作品，參觀者可以在池邊悠遊自在地休息，也可與藝術更親近。

「藝術長廊」走進藝術長廊彷彿走進一處自由而隨性的創作空間。這是一處透過公開徵件的方式，開放給新一代的藝術創作者來現場恣情揮灑，希望能藉此與參觀民眾產生互動的藝術交流，也使「藝術長廊」成為館內一處令人期待的創作空間。

美術館本館《MAIN BUILDING》

朱焦館《JU JUN

太極拱門《TAICHI ARCH》

服務中心《SERVICE CENTER》

天鵝池《SWAN

藝術交流區《INTERCHANGE AREA》

藝術長廊《ARTS C

美術館本館
MAIN BUILDING

人間廣場
LIVING WORLD SQUARE

太極廣場
TAICHI SQUARE

戲水區
PADDLING AREA

藝術交流區
INTERCHANGE AREA

慈母碑
MOTHER MEMORIAL

天鵝池
SWAN POND

藝術長廊
ARTS CORRIDOR

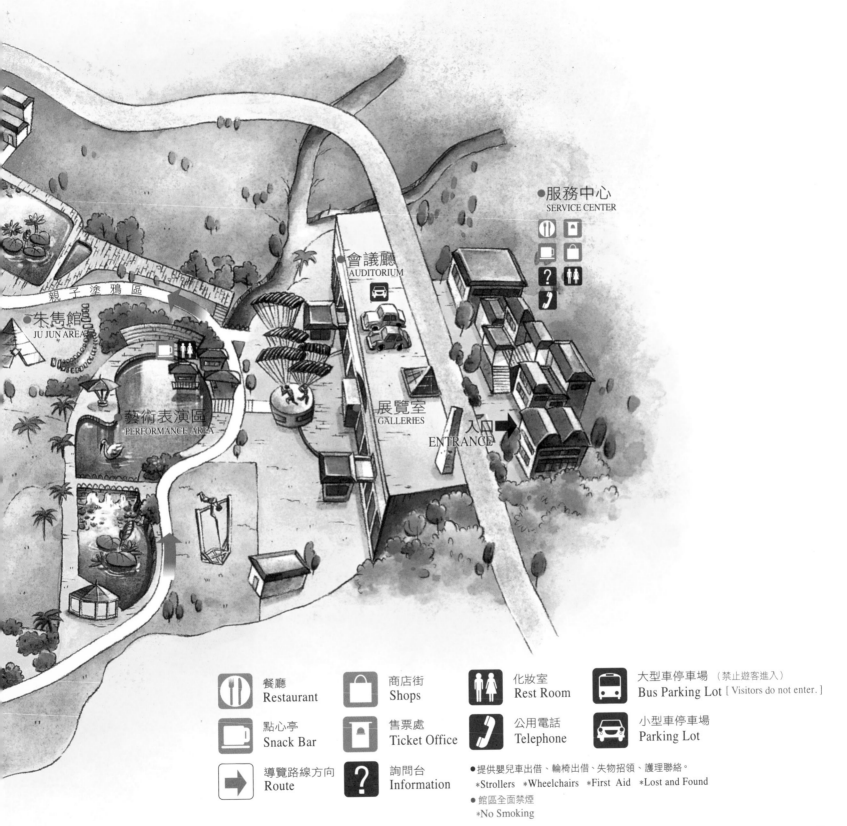

•服務中心
SERVICE CENTER

•會議廳
AUDITORIUM

親子塗鴉區

•朱雋館
JU JUN AREA

藝術表演區
PERFORMANCE AREA

展覽室
GALLERIES

入口
ENTRANCE

| | | | |
|---|---|---|---|
| 餐廳<br>Restaurant | 商店街<br>Shops | 化妝室<br>Rest Room | 大型車停車場（禁止遊客進入）<br>Bus Parking Lot [ Visitors do not enter. ] |
| 點心亭<br>Snack Bar | 售票處<br>Ticket Office | 公用電話<br>Telephone | 小型車停車場<br>Parking Lot |
| 導覽路線方向<br>Route | 詢問台<br>Information | | |

•提供嬰兒車出借、輪椅出借、失物招領、護理聯絡。
*Strollers  *Wheelchairs  *First Aid  *Lost and Found

•館區全面禁煙
*No Smoking

《SERVICE CENTER》 Here you'll find the museum gift shops and a lounge in the Service Center. The gift shops provide a variety of art gifts designed by the museum designing crew and the lounge provides various kinds of delicious food, snacks and beverages. Visitors can choose their gifts and drinks here.

《GALLERIES》 The gallery comprises two-story exhibition space. Multitudes of artworks are constantly on display at the hall; also other artists' works are on display on a temporary basis. Visitors can appreciate many masterpieces by Pablo Ruiz Picasso, Bernard Buffet, Henry Moore, Andy Warhol... and the paintings by representative artists in Taiwan. The Living World Series works focusing on sports are displayed outside the galleries. The largest parachute above the stand was exhibited in Musée d'Art Contemporain de Dunkerque, France in 1991.

《AUDITORIUM》 With the capacity to hold about 300 people, the auditorium may be used for multiple purposes, providing a great meeting place for lectures, symposiums and employee training sessions in a nice, art-oriented environment. Two Ju Ming's works, power shovel, are exhibited in here. These two power shovels were used during the museum in construct. After then, Ju Ming transformed them into his works by re-arranging them and giving them two drivers in Living World Series.

《PERFORMANCE AREA》 The Performance Area is an open-air theater for a variety of performances. Its auditorium comprises coliseum-like arc-shape steps. This area holds different performances on an unscheduled basis. To allow the theatergoers to enjoy his art, a multiple of Ju Ming's Living World Series works made of stainless steel and bronze are positioned on the perimeter of the theater.

《JU JUN AREA》 Ju Jun is Ju Ming's oldest son and a well-known sculptor in Taiwan. His recent works, Zipper Series, are especially outstanding. The area houses three different types of Zipper Series: Crescent-shape Zipper Lotus Pond, Zipper Tent and Zipper Stones.

《POND AREA》 The Pond Area comprises Wish Pond, Lotus Pond and Water Playing Pond. Wish Pond is encircled by stone works of Ju Ming's Living World Series. Ju Ming said that the Wish Pond is like the wish pond in Rome and the stone works encircling it are observing humanity. Nearby, the lotuses in Lotus Pond bloom every summer.

《TAICHI SQUARE》 On the Taichi Square that is full of green grass, over 30 works of Taichi Series are on the display. Most of them are large-size bronze works. Their sheer size and magnificent shapes put visitors in the state of taichi.

《MAIN BUILDING》 The Main Building has the outer appearance of a pyramid. The most impressive part of the building is the fact that the building's exterior is made of stainless steel and bronze. The building houses Ju Ming's earlier works including wood sculptures, painted-wood sculptures and plane painting. Also, two exhibition rooms are chosen to exhibit the works of his two teachers, Lee Chin-chuan and Yuyu Yang to commemorate the tremendous influence and impacts on him from these great teachers.

《LIVING WORLD SQUARE》 The Living World Square displays a multitude of Living World Series that are made mainly of bronze and stone. Along with "Gentlemen", the most conspicuous works are other Living World Series sculptures depicting various forms and stories of the humanity. Ai Bridge, linking the Taichi Square to the Living World Square, was built by Ju Ming to commemorate his mother, Wong Ai.

《INTERCHANGE AREA》 This outdoor square gives the professional artists the opportunity to publish their works through invitation or application from the museum. In addition to enjoy Ju Ming's works in the vastness of the sculpture park, visitors can commune with master works of modern artists in the Interchange Area.

《MOTHER MEMORIAL》 The Mother Memorial was the first area completed in the museum. Many of Ju Ming's works illustrate the deep affection between a mother and her children. The memorial is built to show his affection to his mother and a good representative work which he wants to talk about family relationship in his Living World Series. The other figures surrounding the mother were Ju Ming and his brothers, sisters and friends.

《SWAN POND》 The Swan Pond is provided to the visitors for resting and chatting. The visitors may enjoy watching the real swans or the swans created by Ju Ming swimming in the pond. You can also look at a lot of small-size sculptures in Ju Ming's earlier period.

《ARTS CORRIDOR》 The Arts Corridor is open to new artists so that they may have an opportunity to exhibit their works to the public. The museum hopes to use this place to have an art exchange with the visitors. After we enter this place, we can feel the freedom and creativity of art.

人間廣場《LIVING WORLD SQUARE》

太極廣場《TAICHI AREA》

慈母碑《MOTHER MEMORIAL》

會議室《AUDITORIUM》

展覽室《GALLERIES》

藝術表演區《PERFORMANCE AREA》

戲水區《POND AREA》

67

國家圖書館出版品預行編目資料

朱銘美術館導覽手冊 / 朱銘美術館典藏研究部
編輯統籌. -- 臺北縣金山鄉 ： 朱銘文教基金
會，民91
面 ； 公分

ISBN 986-80266-0-1

1. 朱銘 – 傳記 2. 朱銘美術館 – 手冊,便覽
等

906.8                                        91005350

JUMING MUSEUM

發 行 人＞朱原利
發 行 所＞財團法人朱銘文教基金會
發行日期＞中華民國九十一年四月
地　　址＞208台北縣金山鄉西勢湖2號
電　　話＞886-2-24989940　傳真＞886-2-24988529
網　　址＞http://www.juming.org.tw
編輯統籌＞朱銘美術館 典藏研究部
設　　計＞李記創意股份有限公司
攝　　影＞八澄石／朱雋／高淑媛／陳慶良／趙順景／劉永波
郵政劃撥＞19381371　戶名＞財團法人朱銘文教基金會
售　　價＞新台幣180元

印　　製＞博聞堂彩色印刷有限公司


Publisher > Calvin Ju

Published by > Nonprofit Organization Juming Culture and Education Foundation

Issue Date > 2002. 04.

Tel. > 886-2-24989940　　Fax. > 886-2-24988529

Add. > 208 No. 2 She-shi-hu Chin-shan Taipei, Taiwan, R.O.C.

Website > http://www.juming.org.tw

Edited by > Collection & Research Department of Juming Museum

Designed by > Lee Chi Creativity Co., Ltd.

Photographers > Chao Shuen-chin/ Cheng Ching-liang/ J. H. Johnson Lai/ Ju Jun/ Kao Shu-yuan/ Yung-bo Liu

Post Bank Account No. > 19381371　　Account > Nonprofit Organization Juming Culture and Education Foundation

Price > NT$ 180


Printed by > Doctor House Press Co., Ltd.